better together*

*This book is best read together, grownup and kid.

akidsco.com

a kids book about being an introvert

by Amy Taylor & Josh Maynard

a
kids
book
about

Text and design copyright © 2023
by A Kids Book About, Inc.

Copyright is good! It ensures that work like this can exist, and more work in the future can be created.

All rights reserved. No part of this publication may be reproduced, distributed, or transmitted in any form or by any means, including photocopying, recording, other electronic or mechanical methods, without the prior written permission of the publisher, except in the case of brief quotations embodied in critical reviews and certain other noncommercial uses permitted by copyright law. For permission requests, write to the publisher.

A Kids Book About, Kids Are Ready, and the colophon 'a' are trademarks of A Kids Book About, Inc.

Printed in the United States of America.

A Kids Book About books are available online: *akidsco.com*

To share your stories, ask questions, or inquire about bulk purchases (schools, libraries, and nonprofits), please use the following email address: *hello@akidsco.com*

Print ISBN: 978-1-958825-29-7
Ebook ISBN: 978-1-958825-32-7

Designed by Josh Maynard
Edited by Emma Wolf

This book is dedicated to the "quiet kids" (and grownups) of the world.

We see you.
We love you.
We are you.

Intro

Ask any grownup introvert and they can probably recall struggling to find their voice and place in the world as a kid. There was constant pressure to fit in, speak up, and be someone different.

That's some serious hooey.

This book is filled with the message we needed once upon a time as introvert kids. Our goal is to validate this experience and spark important conversations about introversion between little humans and the big humans who love them.

If you're reading this, it's clear you care deeply about the introverted kid in your life. Whether you personally identify as an introvert, we hope you'll share your experiences and challenges with your kiddo. And we hope they'll feel seen, safe, and supported knowing that while they may savor the occasional solo time, they're never actually alone in the world. (In fact, with almost half the population now identifying as introverts…they're in really great company.)[1]

---

[1]. Francesca Gino, "Introverts, Extroverts, and the Complexities of Team Dynamics," Harvard Business Review, August 12, 2015, https://hbr.org/2015/03/introverts-extroverts-and-the-complexities-of-team-dynamics.

Have you ever heard someone say...

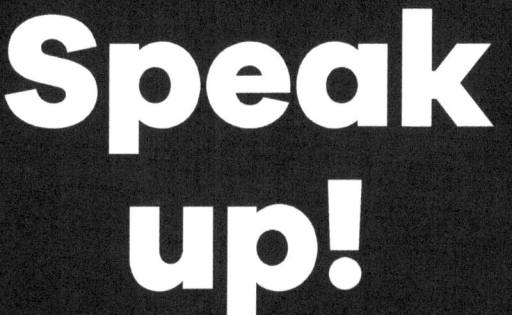

Part of growing up means exploring what it means to be...

uniqu

ely
you.

But these kinds of words can make you doubt yourself, or feel like you need to pretend to be someone you're not.

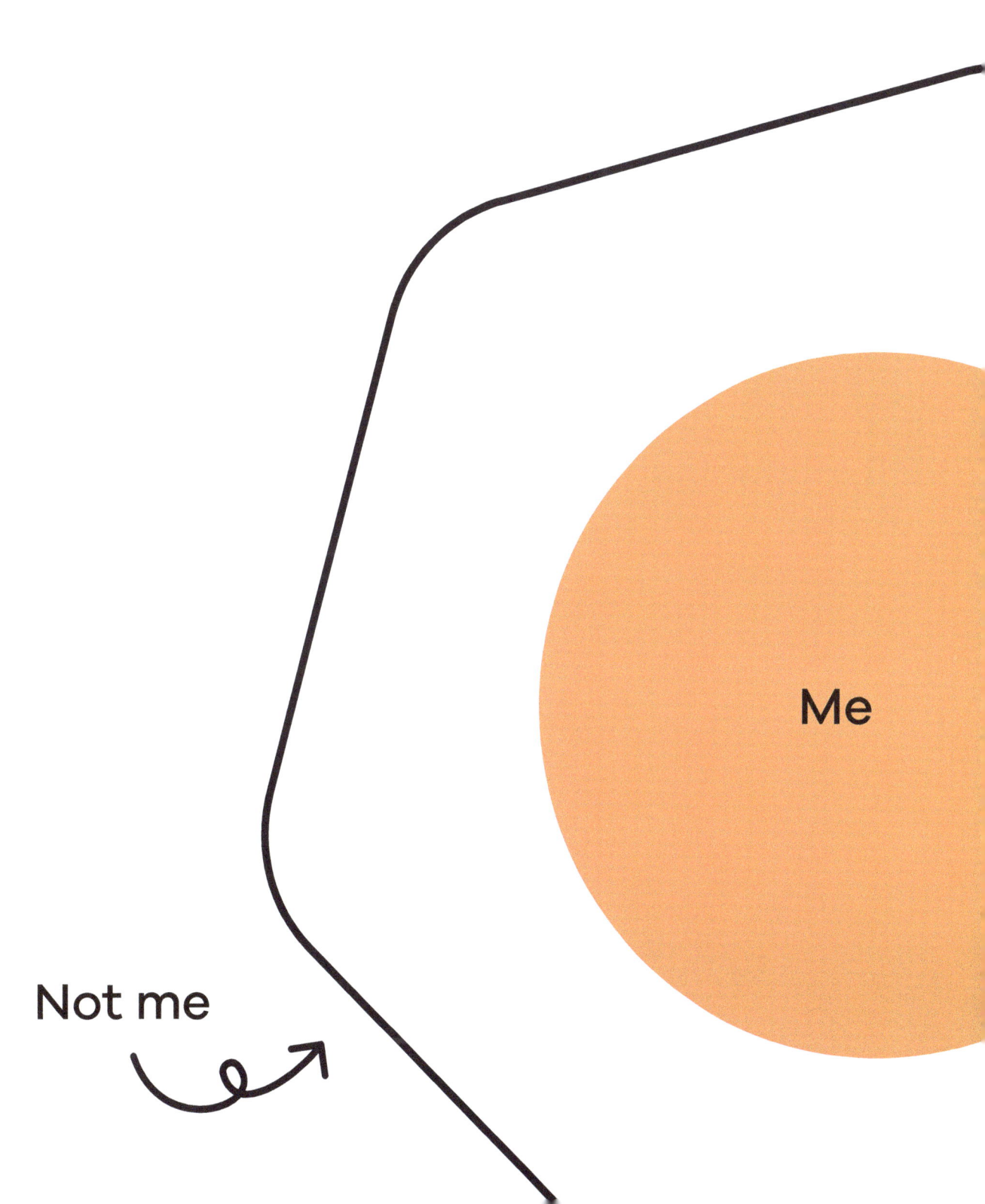

This book is
for introverts
and exists to

celeb

rate

the "quiet kids" of the world.

Hello! We're Amy and Josh. This is our book about being introverts.

I'm Amy!

I'm a writer, storyteller, introvert, and proud dog mom.

PRO TIP: Sometimes it might be easier to express your thoughts and feelings in writing than it is in chatty conversation. That's lovely! Words can be just as powerful and magical when written as they are when spoken.

I'm Josh!

I'm a dad to 3 tiny humans, a web and brand designer, and an introvert also.

PRO TIP: When I'm feeling uncomfortable at a party or event, I always look for a pet. Nothing calms my nerves quite like spending time with a cute pup!

And there are sooo many others just like us.

Here are just a few of the roles fellow introverts have filled throughout history:

 **Iconic actors**
(like Emma Watson)

 **Record-breaking athletes**
(like Michael Jordan)

 **Inspiring world leaders**
(like Barack Obama)

 **Big thinkers**
(like Albert Einstein)

 **and some pretty great friends**
(like you!)

So you might be asking yourself...

Am intro

I an vert?

(What even *is* an introvert?)

We could probably fill 101 books explaining what it means to be an introvert. (Like these!)

- **The Invisible Boy** by Trudy Ludwig
- **Gustavo the Shy Ghost** by Flavia Z. Drago
- **KINDergarten** by Vera Ahiyya
- **Shy** by Deborah Freedman
- **Shy Dog: A Children's Book about Overcoming Shyness and Being Brave** by Karen Kilpatrick

But to put it as simply as we can...

- **Love Birds** by Jane Yolen
- **How to Party Like a Snail** by Naseem Hrab
- **A Way with Wild Things** by Larissa Theule
- **I Am Quiet: A Story for the Introvert in All of Us** by Andie Powers
- **Captain Starfish** by Davina Bell

An introvert is someone who tends to enjoy spending time alone and might feel a little bit overwhelmed in crowds or social situations.

Introverts are often called...

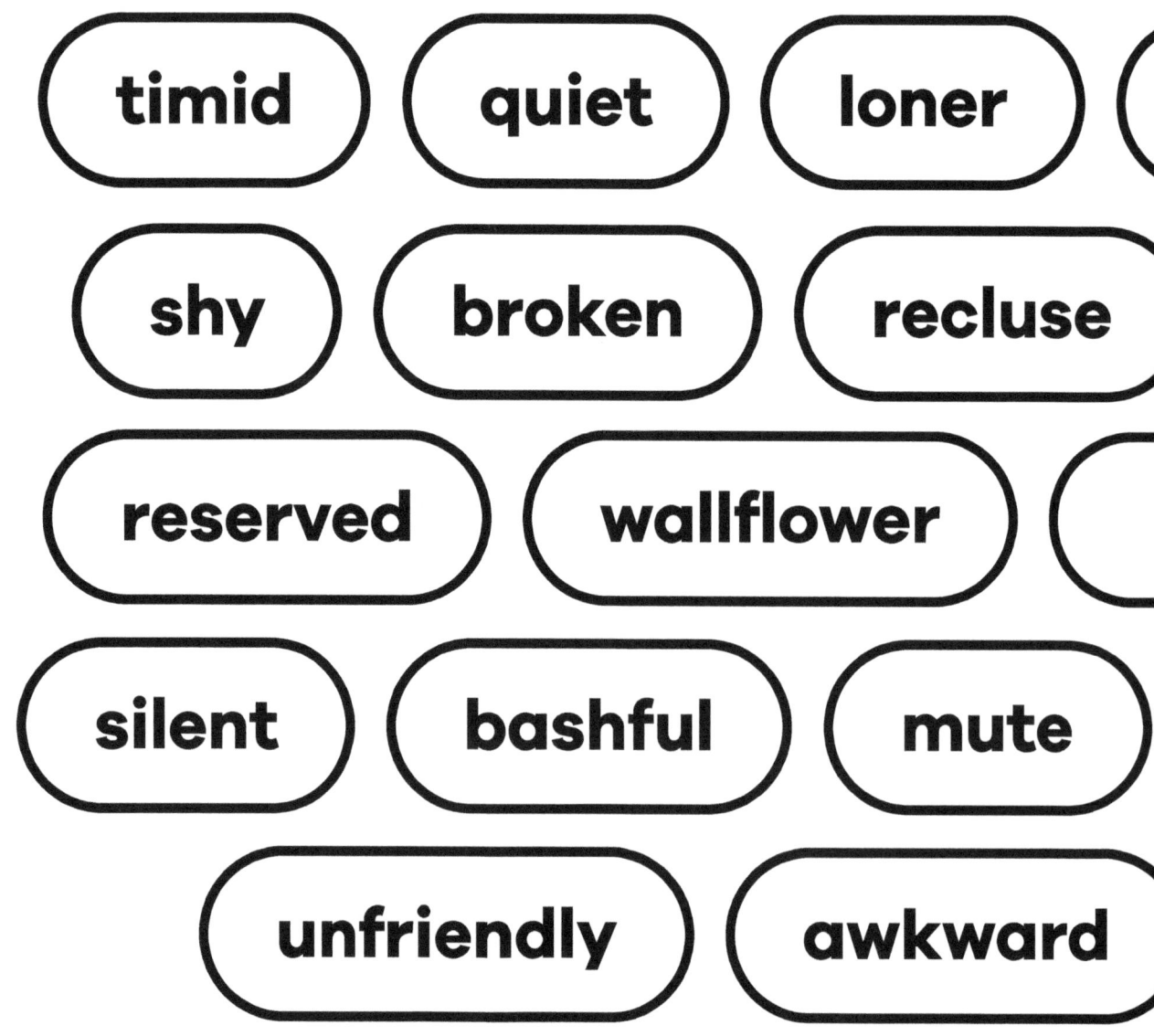

timid · quiet · loner · shy · broken · recluse · reserved · wallflower · silent · bashful · mute · unfriendly · awkward

anti-social   skeptic

aloof   solitary   hermit

detached   boring

homebody   strange

nerdy   or   withdrawn.

Have you ever been called any of those names?

It probably felt **terrible**.

You may have felt **left out** or **misunderstood**.

These kinds of words can even make us wonder if something is **wrong with us**.

But those names are not who you are and don't define you.

Being an introvert is so much more than **labels.**

And it's actually pretty incredible.

Take it from us, introverts are some of the most...

creative, thoughtful, courageous, and loyal people.

And chances are,
if you're reading this...

you might be

Hi!

So what makes an introvert... an introvert?

Well, introverts are:

1

Good listeners.

We're always here for you, especially when you're hurting or struggling.

2. Loyal friends.

We'll stick by you through thick and thin.

3. Big thinkers.

We're full of creative thoughts and amazing ideas.

4

Really considerate.

We always think before speaking or acting.

5

Super independent.

We create fun even when we're on our own.

*Even still!

Other people don't always understand what it's like to be an introvert, though.

Sometimes introverts...

would rather hang out alone than with friends.

need a quiet spot to recharge their batteries.

need extra time to think before answering a question.

take time getting to know someone before being completely comfortable around them.

All of those things are **fine**, **good**, and **normal**.

Every kid is different!

Some kids love performing on stage.

Some kids have lots of friends.

Some kids feel really excited about meeting new friends on the first day of school.

But for some introverts, it feels scary— even impossible.

Some introverts prefer 1 or 2 friends they know really, really well.

And some introverts are happiest at home reading their favorite book.

This is me!

There are so many different ways to be human.

There's no right or wrong.

It's about what makes you feel **safe** and **secure**.

And because each of us is so unique, that can look sooooo different.

introvert

And that's OK!

———— **extrovert**

So if you're a fellow introvert, we've got some important things to tell you.

Listen up!

It's perfectly fine to say no to a sleepover or overnight camp if you don't feel comfortable.

If it feels overwhelming to raise your hand often in class, talk to your teachers about other ways of sharing your answers—maybe through writing!

You don't need to hang out in a group if you'd rather spend time with a friend one-on-one.

Don't worry about trying to be like everyone else.

Know that what others may think about you or call you does not define you.

If you feel like you might be an introvert, we think these words are a much more accurate description of your superpowers...

- kind
- curious
- patient
- intelligent
- considerate
- thoughtful
- observant
- understanding
- helpful

creative gentle deep introspective interesting respectful empathetic caring and amazing!

By being true to your introverted self, you make the world a…

kinder, better place where everyone feels safe, accepted, & welcome.

Exactly as
they are.

Outro

Hello again, grownups. This book is just the beginning of a much bigger (and very important) conversation about the value of introverts and how we can advocate for the introverts in our lives.

But don't fret! Fostering introvert inclusivity can be as simple as offering alternate ways of doing things to make our introverted kiddos feel seen, safe, and supported so they can fully shine.

If you notice your kid feeling overwhelmed or overstimulated at a social gathering, help them find a quiet spot to take a breather. If you have students in your class who hesitate to raise their hand, consider integrating a written option for sharing their thoughts. The possibilities are endless. One thing that's certain? They'll never forget what it feels like knowing you're on their side.

Looking for additional resources? All of the books from the earlier illustration are real!

About The Authors & Illustrator

Amy Taylor (she / her) is an Ohio-based writer and storyteller. As a kid, she was a certified chatterbox, but that started to feel like wearing socks 3 sizes too small as she aged into adulthood. Today, she's a proud introvert (and Hufflepuff) who feels most like herself when spending time with her family, rescue dog, and garden.

 writehuman.com

Josh Maynard (he / him) is a designer in Arvada, Colorado, with a focus on creating more accessible web experiences for all. As a lifelong introvert and a dad to 3 (boisterous) tiny humans, he has the incredible challenge of finding much-needed time to recharge his introvert batteries while managing the ever-present to-do list that comes with dad duty.

 @joshmaynard.co   joshmaynard.co

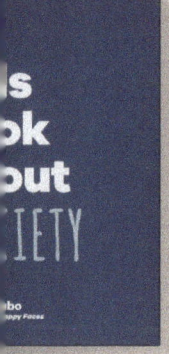

Discover more at akidsco.com

www.ingramcontent.com/pod-product-compliance
Lightning Source LLC
Chambersburg PA
CBHW062023050526
44107CB00106B/982